T0128412

TRUST YOUR FEELINGS!

Why It Matters

DR. ROBERT OBOL NYEKO

authorHOUSE®

AuthorHouse™
1663 Liberty Drive
Bloomington, IN 47403
www.authorhouse.com
Phone: 1 (800) 839-8640

Published by AuthorHouse   07/30/2019

ISBN: 978-1-7283-1428-0 (sc)
ISBN: 978-1-7283-1427-3 (hc)
ISBN: 978-1-7283-1441-9 (e)

Library of Congress Control Number: 2019907112

Print information available on the last page.

Any people depicted in stock imagery provided by Getty Images are models, and such images are being used for illustrative purposes only. Certain stock imagery © Getty Images.

This book is printed on acid-free paper.

To my personal friends, who have

never cheated on me.

CONTENTS

Acknowledgments ix

Introduction xiii

Chapter 1   Feelings Predict the Future 1

Chapter 2   Feelings Are a Reliable Basis for Life

Commitment 5

Chapter 3   Mothers Making Health Care

Decisions Based on Feelings 9

Chapter 4   Feelings Speak to Family Members

about Other Members 13

Chapter 5   Feelings Warn of Life–Changing Events... 21

Chapter 6   Feelings Communicate What May

Happen at the Workplace 27

Chapter 7   Feelings Alert One to Possible Danger 31

Chapter 8   Feelings Tell When One Is Ready for

a Break 39

Chapter 9   Feelings Reveal Hostility in the Air 41

Chapter 10 Feelings Provide Clarity When Faced

with Tough Choices 47

Chapter 11 The Power of Feelings to Show Care

for Others 51

Chapter 12 My Feelings Communicate When It

Is Time to Move On 57

Chapter 13 Dogs Also Trust Their Feelings 61

Conclusion 65

Appendix 69

About the Author 83

ACKNOWLEDGMENTS

This is my second book. The first book I published was titled *The Life and Lessons from a Warzone: A Memoir of Dr. Robert Obol Nyeko.* In writing these two books, I have learned something about the personal discipline needed to be a successful writer. Anyone can be a writer, a reviewer, or an editor, but the distinguishing mark is passion and commitment.

I would like to thank my editor, William Skoluda. When working on any project, Bill gives his whole heart and all of his time. His world revolves around it. And this one has been no exception. I believe that he is among the best in the business.

I want to thank Donna Caputo for her observations.

Donna always brings her wisdom and a fresh eye to what I have written. I am happy to say that she has been part of my writing projects for almost a decade now, beginning with my doctoral dissertation and then my first book and now my second.

I also wish to thank Mr. Al Henagar, the clinical pastoral education supervisor of the University of Kansas Health System. Mr. Henagar has a deep reservoir of knowledge about human behavior. Among the many things that he teaches aspiring chaplains is that they need to be in touch with their own personal feelings if they are to be effective in the profession. His observation that this work could make a significant contribution to the appreciation of human feelings and his encouragement gave me great confidence about the direction I was taking and the choices I made as I wrote.

I express my appreciation to Fr. Melvin Rusnak for his friendship and support. Fr. Melvin was the contrarian or the skeptic throughout this process. He asked many thought-provoking questions that made me think through and refine my thoughts on the subject of feelings.

I am also grateful to Jill Michaud, and I thank her for her critical analysis of this book. I particularly appreciate her suggestions to move certain sections of the book and to make additions that brought clarity and completeness.

I also thank Sr. Grace Aciro for being part of this journey. I am so grateful that I could count on her enthusiasm, availability, and encouragement as I worked on this project. Just as she did with the first book, she guided me through the many traps encountered when writing in proper English.

Finally, I am grateful to Dr. David Kimori for coming on this journey without any hesitation. His fresh perspective will be of great benefit to those who will now be encountering my writing for the first time. I look forward to working with him on many projects in the years to come.

INTRODUCTION

I have written this book because I want to demonstrate how often we are influenced by our feelings, for I believe they play a much bigger role in our lives than we tend to realize.

The format of this book uses short narratives. The topics include how feelings contribute to self-awareness and awareness of the environment; the role feelings play in good decision-making; how feelings bring clarity to confusing situations; the role of feelings in establishing emotional connections; and, above all, the great potential that people have yet to explore in the sphere of feelings through personal reflection and discovery.

Over time, I have spoken with numerous individuals

about the role of feelings in their lives, including members of my family, health care leaders, salespersons, social workers, pastoral agents, and my coworkers. When dealing with members of their immediate family, many of them indicated that they relied primarily on their feelings.

In this book, I make distinctions between feelings and emotions. I define emotions as instinctive and physical; they evoke immediate bodily reactions to a threat, a reward, or perhaps even an unexpected compliment. They are chemicals released in our body in response to a certain trigger. Emotional reactions are rooted in our genes and, in short, are responses to a stimulus.

Feelings are about something we sense. Feelings are about perceiving an emotion and assigning a value to it—for example, to consider something as important and worthy of attention or as insignificant and unworthy of attention. Feelings arise when we begin to assimilate an emotion by thinking about it and letting it sink in.

Feelings are therefore a person's mental associations with and reactions to an emotion. But feelings go deeper than emotions, because they can last much longer in individuals. By contrast, intuition is the ability of a person to read and to interpret their feelings accurately.

I strongly believe that when it comes to good decision-making, there is a need for the integration of our feelings and our intellect, because it can be problematic if one operates at the extremes, either relying mostly on the intellect or relying primarily on feelings. Good decisions are a product of both.

For example, a person may experience a strong fear of the unknown, but sometimes this fear has a legitimate basis. It could be due to past mistakes or mishaps. This fear is tempered by the intellect, which raises questions so that the person becomes balanced and does not become paranoid.

As part of my college education, I studied philosophy.

Its focus was on intellectual training and developing my ability to explain things logically and rationally. Feelings were often considered unreliable and thus of limited value. However, in real life, my feelings have been the foundation for some of the best and most durable decisions I have ever made. My long-term commitments have my feelings written all over them.

Further, I believe that even though many people consider feelings to be vague and unformed, they can bring clarity to conflicting situations because those who understand the patterns of their feelings know exactly how to react when they realize they are experiencing a particular feeling.

As a professional pastoral counselor and a spiritual-care provider, I have found that often a situation will arise where words have their limitations in expressing compassion and care. It is in such situations that nonverbally sharing in others' feelings of pain creates a connection with people at a much deeper level than words ever could.

Therefore, feelings should not be looked at in isolation; instead, people should strive to make associations between what they feel and what they see and hear. This can give us a more complete picture of a situation.

Moreover, people should pay greater attention to how they feel in particular situations. If they are stressed, they should examine the range of feelings they experience. It could be body pain, constant forgetfulness, sleeplessness, or inattention. If they master the patterns of their feelings and their bodily reactions to these situations, they will be better able to read and interpret the messages their feelings are communicating to them.

As a young priest, I worked at Pajule parish in Northern Uganda, which was at the epicenter of a war between the Lord's Resistance Army (LRA) and the government of Uganda. Ninety-eight percent of the time, there was not enough information available to determine if it would be safe to act as I wished to, especially if I needed to travel. Usually, I had to rely on my feelings. In this book, I share many of the decisions that I made based on those feelings.

While the focus of this book is on human feelings, I would also like to say that animals have feelings as well, clearly shown in how they relate with human beings. Their behaviors show a deeper degree of awareness beyond the merely casual.

As I share my life experiences, my hope is that they open a window into your life about your own feelings and contribute to a greater degree of self-awareness, so that you may better appreciate what your feelings are communicating to you and recognize that tuning into your feelings helps you make good decisions.

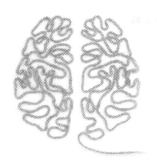

FEELINGS PREDICT THE FUTURE

When I grew up as a young boy in Uganda in the early 1980s, the northern part of the country where I lived with my family was peaceful. The central part of the country, specifically the Luwero Triangle, was not peaceful, and later the southwestern parts of the country also became uncontrollable. It was commonplace to hear of attacks by rebels on government soldiers, travelers, and other innocent parties.

The National Resistance Army (NRA) was the name taken by the rebels battling the government of Dr. Apollo Milton Obote and later that of Gen. Tito Okello Lutwa. The northern part of Uganda remained mostly peaceful, but there was always a certain feeling of looming disaster, as if any peace in the North could not last if a change in government were to occur. Many wanted to believe that there was no credible way the rebels could take power; they were seen as a disgruntled group who were power hungry and the sore losers of an election that had been held in 1980. Despite the uneasiness, most people thought the NRA had almost no chance of overthrowing the government.

However, on January 26, 1986, the National Resistance Movement did assume power, and Northern Uganda became embroiled in armed conflict for close to twenty-five years. What the average person had been fearing for a long time became a reality as violence and uncertainty came to define their daily lives.

I share this story because many of the catastrophes that have taken place were foreseen; this can be understood by examining the events of a particular historical period and the feelings that prevailed.

For example, the generation of the 1930s witnessed the rise of Hitler and the coming to power of the Nazis in Germany. They sensed something was not right when they saw the German leader become a dictator and act outside the rule of law and their national constitution, as thuggery and even murder became commonplace. They could feel something unsettling in the air along with a sense of gloom and a feeling that a dark period was coming, which was confirmed by the eventual outbreak of the Second World War, the destruction of Germany and Europe, and the loss of millions of lives.

Consider that in our lifetime, the most traumatic event that we witnessed was September 11, 2001. Probably only the terrorists who planned it knew that the attack was going to happen. However, there were prevailing feelings in the air as well. There was uneasiness surrounding what the consequences would be for humanity, as religion was increasingly being used as a vehicle for mass murder.

The strange and frightening feelings about the distortion of religion were a precursor to the barbaric and horrific terrorist attacks on the United States on September, 11, 2001. I strongly believe that prevailing feelings of a particular period capture and precede what then takes place.

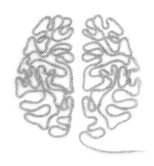

2

FEELINGS ARE A RELIABLE BASIS FOR LIFE COMMITMENT

After completing my high school education, I needed to decide what to do with the rest of my life. Intellectually, I had two choices: to be a Catholic priest or not. To be a Catholic priest meant that I would have no family of my own, I might receive assignments far from home, and my bishop would be the one to tell me what was best for me.

I also thought about the life of a lay person, which held the possibility of getting married, having children, and leading a life of independence. I kept bouncing back and forth between these two choices. On one day, I tended toward the ministry, and the following day, I leaned to the life of a lay person.

All this introspection did not provide me with the clear-cut answer I was looking for. What I found most reliable were my feelings, which consistently told me that I should be a Catholic priest. The thought of becoming a priest provided me with the peace and calm I sought and, above all, a sense of belonging. And now, even after eighteen years, the stability of my calling as a priest is grounded in those feelings.

It is my belief that when people consider entering into a lifetime commitment, such as marriage, they need to consider the messages their feelings are conveying before deciding to proceed. If their feelings confirm their thoughts, it may indicate that their choice is right for them, and they will be at peace with the decision. But if there is a conflict between a person's thinking and their feelings, there's a good chance that, without deep reflection, the person might go on to lead a life that is conflicted and lacks inner peace. For example, if a person thinks it is time to get married, but their feelings tell them this is not the right person to settle down with, it may require that they press the pause button.

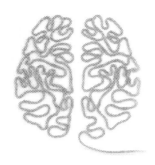

MOTHERS MAKING HEALTH CARE DECISIONS BASED ON FEELINGS

As part of my research, I talked to mothers about caring for infants and children who were unable to clearly articulate their needs and wants. At my former workplace in Uganda, a woman I will call Goretti had given birth to seventeen children. She told me that she had to learn to read every one of her children's individual personalities. When they were sick with an ailment, they all showed different symptoms.

Many times, Goretti relied on what her feelings told her. If the message she received was that the child was sick and needed to be taken to a hospital, that is exactly what she did. And when test results were analyzed, most of the time, her feelings were confirmed.

In the United States, I talked to a woman in her thirties, whom I will call Gloria. She lives in the state of Wisconsin and is raising three children. Gloria told me that she consults her family doctor on all medical decisions pertaining to her children, but even if she receives the best advice on their medical care, her feelings are so important to her that they determine what she considers to be necessary in the medical care of her children.

She says that they tell her what procedures should be prioritized, and the family doctor recommends any elective surgeries. Her feelings determine whether or not to proceed. She recalls many occasions when she ignored sound medical advice due to her feelings.

This also extends to her choice of physicians to care for the medical needs of her children. It is not their expertise or experience that she considers to be most important but rather their ability to connect with her on an emotional level. She needs to like them, have warm feelings toward them, and love to be around them.

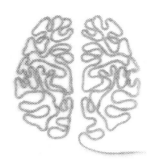

FEELINGS SPEAK TO FAMILY MEMBERS ABOUT OTHER MEMBERS

An insurance executive told me that because his wife had a quiet personality, he relied largely on what his feelings told him to help understand both her and the children and when he needed to make crucial family decisions.

A gentleman who had been married three times told of his second wife, with whom he had felt a special bond. They both worked, so they would usually meet at a restaurant for dinner. Most of the time, his wife was the first to arrive, and she would order their meal without consulting him. On all occasions, what she chose for him was exactly what he had a desire for.

I also talked with a lady in her early fifties about her childhood growing up in the former Soviet Union. She told me that from the age of four to eleven, she could not be raised by her parents because of what was occurring within the country. It was her grandmother, Krupskaya, who took care of her. As a result, she and her grandmother formed a special bond. This bond made her understand exactly what her feelings were saying about her grandmother. When she returned home, she would let her parents know whenever Krupskaya was coming to visit. At first, they questioned where she got her information, because the grandmother never informed anyone of her plans until she actually arrived. When the family saw that their daughter's predictions always came true, if she told them that Krupskaya was on the way, they trusted her and prepared for her arrival.

In my own family, my great-grandmother on the maternal side could feel in her body when my mother,

her granddaughter, Mary Tina, was sick. In her case, it was to the degree of an intuition, since it was not just a vague and constant feeling of unease; she knew exactly what was happening. She would wake up in the morning and tell everyone that Mary Tina needed her. This was in the era before cell phones or any other form of instant communication. She would then take the bus from Gulu to Kitgum, a trip of one hour, and find her to be sick.

On the other hand, my mother, Mary Tina, senses and intuits hardships, illness, and dangers in my life. For example, at the height of the insecurity in November 2003, when I was stationed in Pajule, she once called me out of the blue and asked, "My son, where are you?"

This surprised me because she had never before asked such a direct question! After all, I was an adult and living on my own. I told her that I was on my way back to Pajule parish. I had stopped to visit a senior clergyman at Aboke Trading Center and would soon continue on my journey.

Her sense that I might possibly encounter danger was proven to be correct. On the way to Pajule, I learned that a passenger vehicle traveling before me had been fired on, presumably by rebels.

When I reached the spot where it had occurred, by the roadside I saw government soldiers who had responded to the situation. When I got back to Pajule, I met worried people who were surprised to see another vehicle following immediately after the one that had been ambushed. It could have been me, given the timing.

On another occasion, in November 2015, while working as a hospital chaplain in the US, I saw a doctor because I felt sick. I was given some medication, but the following day, I felt much worse. I did not inform anyone in Uganda, especially my parents.

Perhaps not unexpectedly, I got a call from my mother, who asked, "My son, are you sick?" My mother raised nine children. She cared for us when we were sick and could not speak for ourselves. She learned each of our individual traits and personalities. This was how she mastered her own feelings about each child and was able to sense if a particular one was in danger or unwell.

I am certain that before she called me, a feeling led her to immediately think of me. Here are some of the feelings that she experiences before reaching that intuitive moment about a child: She begins to think of a particular child much more than usual. She feels that child needs her protection, that she needs to pray for the protection of that child from danger. She will find herself saying the rosary for the safety of the child. Finally, she feels a strong urge to reach out to the child, using whatever means possible to find out if he is okay. I believe that these feelings tell her to contact me when I am unwell or in danger.

I also feel something when my father is sick. When I was a student at the seminary, in the first week of May

2000, I had no appetite for several days. I could barely take any breakfast, lunch, or supper. Yet I was not sick. I stopped joining my fellow students for my favorite sport of volleyball in the afternoon and remained in bed, extending my siesta till five o'clock in the evening. I could feel that something was not right but could not place a finger on it.

That very week, the principal of the seminary called and said, "Robert, there is a serious problem! Please, come see me immediately."

I went to his office, where he informed me that my father was at home in Kitgum and was very sick. My mother was asking my sister, a student at Makerere University at the time, and me to leave school before the end of the term so that we could go be with her and my father.

When I heard this, the restlessness within me disappeared, because I understood what the source had been. The following day, I left with my sister to be with our parents. Fortunately, after a long two months, my father recovered.

In December 2006, while visiting a friend in Warren, Ohio, I again experienced restlessness, a lack of appetite, and difficulty in resting or falling asleep. Yet I did not feel physically sick. After three days, I remembered feeling the same way in the year 2000.

I called home to find out how my father was. I talked with my mother, and she informed me that my father had been very sick for the past three days with malaria and was now much better. I know that I can feel my father's health condition since he and I are members of the same family, and I have now mastered a pattern that enables me to read the messages in my body.

All in all, I believe that family members can feel what some of the other members may be going through, and they need to learn how to determine who are the ones with whom they have a unique and special connection.

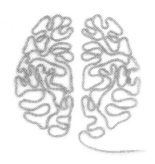

5

FEELINGS WARN OF LIFE–CHANGING EVENTS

On January 23, 2003, Pajule parish where I was stationed as an associate pastor was attacked by the Lord's Resistance Army (LRA). During the many years I had spent in the seminary and the short time I had been a priest, I had never before come face-to-face with death.

For almost one full week, I had no real appetite, though I was not sick. I told the cook not to prepare dinner. In the evening, I would take a cup of warm milk and go to bed, but I could not fall asleep. I normally lost my appetite or could not sleep only when I was unwell or troubled by something. My feelings were telling me something was terribly wrong, and this feeling was so unnatural that everything in me had come to a complete standstill. I knew there was a message being conveyed to me, but I could not put my finger on it.

The day before the attack, a priest who was a member of the Acoli Religious Leaders' Peace Initiative, a local organization that advocated peace and dialogue, arrived at the parish and informed me that the rebels had left the Gulu region and moved nearby into the vicinity of Pajule parish. This surprised me because, until now, we had not been aware of any local rebel activity.

On the morning of the day of the attack, the chairperson of the parish came to visit me, and we soon found ourselves talking about the rapidly deteriorating security situation. When I told her that I felt as if I would soon be abducted by rebels, she said, "Please, Father, do not entertain such thoughts. All will be fine."

Around lunchtime, another gentleman, who was the

peace contact person for the area, arrived at the parish and informed us that he had met the rebel commanders, and indeed they were close by. He had hand-delivered to them a letter from the Acoli religious leaders about the resumption of dialogue.

That afternoon, I followed my habit of taking a nap but again could not fall asleep. I kept turning restlessly and decided to join the social workers at the reception center within the compound of the parish. There, I complained to them that I could neither rest nor sleep, and even in their company, I felt bored and decided to go play volleyball with the returnees.

After the game, I went to take a shower, and that was when the attack began. I now believe that my body had been warning me about the coming attack, but I ignored the associations between my feelings and everything else going on around me at the time.

Two people were killed. The rebels burned the vehicle

parked in the parish garage, which set part of the roof of the rectory on fire. The parish itself was looted, and scores of people were abducted from the town. I spent the night in the bushes for the first time in my life, after running out of the parish house. This event forever changed not only my life but those of many others as well.

It seems that for several weeks, my feelings had been communicating something to me via the restlessness and loss of appetite. I had failed to make the logical connections between my own feelings that we might be attacked and the revelatory signs in my surroundings. First, the confirmation by the priest representative of the Acoli religious leaders that the rebels were in the area of Pajule. Second, the acknowledgment by the peace contact person that he had met the rebel commanders in the area. Third, the rebels had concealed their presence by not engaging in any attacks in the immediate vicinity. If I had trusted my feelings and made connections with all that I was seeing, I probably would have warned those who could to flee and left the parish house long before the rebels besieged it.

I believe there is a lesson that we can all draw from this. We often find ourselves in situations in which we feel paralyzed—meaning we cannot decide for or against something because our feelings are neither clear enough nor forceful enough to pursue a particular course of action. Suppose one would like to end a relationship that is no longer mutually beneficial. In my view, one should not rely only on one's feelings to make a decision. I suggest that the person also ask of themselves this question: "What do I see?" Sometimes, the fact that the relationship is irreparable is in plain sight; there is no trust, no goodwill, and no effort being made to repair it.

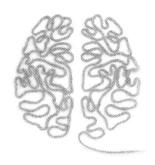

6

FEELINGS COMMUNICATE WHAT MAY HAPPEN AT THE WORKPLACE

I have talked to many people who said they relied on their personal feelings to interpret the atmosphere in their workplace. A friend that I will call Conrad told me that he relies on his feelings to understand his superiors and coworkers and to tell him if a coworker might be having a hard time on the job. Others experienced certain unique feelings before they lost their jobs.

I agree with the view that feelings communicate to us about our workplace. During the time I was in Pajule, I was also the chaplain of the reception center in Pajule and

Pader Town. In April 2004, I celebrated Sunday Mass in the parish church and then had lunch and took a siesta.

Afterward, I felt uneasy and low spirited. I decided to go to Pajule town to socialize with other people and have a drink, thinking that it might lighten my mood, but it didn't. Even the company of friends did not make me feel better. I returned to the parish downcast and went to bed but could not sleep.

After I got up in the morning and said Mass, I still did not feel like my usual self. I had no energy or desire to face the new day. I was bored, tired, and unenthusiastic. Above all, I had no sense of purpose. After breakfast, I went back to bed and did not go to my office.

At around ten thirty in the morning, I got out of bed, as I had planned to make a fifteen-minute drive to a place called Oguta on Lira—Kitgum Road, from which I could place a call to Gulu and make arrangements to service my vehicle. As soon as I left the house, a social worker ran toward me and informed me that the accountant of the Pader Town Catholic Charities Office had been killed.

As soon as I heard this, the restlessness within me ceased. In fact, my feelings had been telling me that death was in the air. I realized that whenever I experienced a restlessness that I considered extraordinary, along with intense turmoil inside me, it was a pointer to something unpleasant yet to come.

The accountant had been traveling with the driver and the accountant of the Pajule reception center when he was shot and killed by rebels at a place called Paiula on Pajule—Pader Road. Fortunately, the other two employees were able to drive through the gunfire unharmed.

I believe I had feelings of restlessness foreshadowing what was to happen because I had a close relationship with each of the social workers and the accountant who was killed. I am convinced that when people develop deep ties with their coworkers, the means of communication with one another broadens beyond the usual verbal, electronic, and handwritten communications.

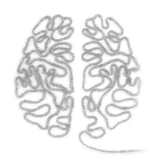

7

FEELINGS ALERT ONE TO POSSIBLE DANGER

I woke up early one morning during the wartime to go to Pader Town, which was about fifteen minutes away from Pajule parish. After I ate breakfast, I was ready to go.

As I left Pajule, I told the townspeople I had to attend an important meeting in Pader Town with the district leaders but was very uneasy about this trip because my emotional reaction to this particular journey was not to travel.

In this book, I speak about the distinction between emotions and feelings, and I have defined emotions as instinctive and physical, while feelings are about something we can sense. I have already told of days when I was to travel and had feelings of uncertainty that caused me to adjust my plans accordingly. But this day, I had to deal with my emotions. And in this case, the emotion I felt was extreme fear, because I was so uncertain I would be able to travel safely to Pader Town.

As I approached a place on the road called Paiula, which was considered to be very unsafe, I saw an army truck parked in the middle of the road and wondered if the truck had been hit by the LRA. But then I remembered that I had not heard of any attacks that day.

I was unsure about proceeding until I saw soldiers lying under the truck, trying to repair it, while others guarded the vehicle. Two civilians appeared from behind the truck and asked me if the road ahead was safe, and I told them that to my knowledge it was and continued on to Pader Town.

Whenever I went to Pader, I stopped at the office of

Catholic Charities since it was an arm of the Catholic Church in the area. On this occasion, I did not stay but left immediately for my meeting. The district leaders asked me questions about conditions on the road from Pajule to Pader Town, but I had no real information to impart to them.

After the meeting, I immediately returned to the office of Catholic Charities, and as always, the coordinator wanted to take me out for lunch, but this time I turned him down. I told him that I wanted to leave immediately for Pajule because I had the same fear inside me about the safety of the road as I did when I traveled to Pader Town.

As I headed back, I worried about passing through Paiula. As I neared it, I saw grass burning and concluded it must be government soldiers, because the rebels would not burn the grass but instead use it for camouflage if they staged an ambush. Indeed, they were government soldiers. I greeted them, but they did not answer.

I continued on my journey, and when I reached a place called Ogan about five minutes away from Pajule, I saw two men riding their bicycles toward Pader Town and waved to them as I passed by. When I later reached the parish, a social worker came up to me and asked, "Father, how did you pass through Ogan? We have just received information that the rebels are waylaying people there."

In response, I put on a brave face, tried to remain as calm as possible, and told him I had made it safely. At the same time, I felt sick to my stomach because I knew I could very well have been one of the victims. I got some consolation by telling myself that this was part of the daily price I had to pay to accomplish something good in a warzone.

After a siesta, I heard that the rebels had killed the two bicycle riders I encountered, and days later, I learned that when news of the killings broke in Pader Town, many people thought I could have been one of the victims, since

I was the only person they knew of who had left Pader Town for Pajule that day. I believe that the emotional anxiety I experienced on my journey from Pajule to Pader Town was a message to me and that my choice to refuse lunch in Pader Town might have saved my life.

How could this event invite you to have a greater reliance on and form a greater appreciation of your own feelings and emotions? Some of us believe in the idea of a good day and a bad day. A good day is a day when one's plans succeed, and a bad day is when many of the things a person plans fail. I believe it all starts with how one feels when they wake up in the morning. One's feelings often foreshadow what is to come on that particular day.

For some who believe in the concept of a good day, how their day starts is usually a good indication of what is to come. When they wake up in the morning, they can feel it will be a special day. As they get out of bed, they feel upbeat, energized, and happy. Some find themselves doing things that they do not often do, like singing aloud in the shower, and others find themselves listening to their favorite music. When they report about the success of the day, they remember it all started with a feeling of optimism and anticipation.

Those who believe in the concept of a bad day remember how dispirited their waking up in the morning was. They recall not wanting to get out of bed, and if they did, they got out of bed late. The usual amount of energy they had when they woke up felt depleted, and everything seemed to move slowly for them that day.

I share with you the story of a thirty-eight-year-old woman I will call Vienna. Vienna had a spotless driving record. On this particular day, she woke up feeling lazy and tired. She had an important meeting she needed to attend, and she was tempted to call and report that she was not coming. At the last minute, she opted to go.

She drove to the venue of the meeting using the same routes she had driven for the last four years. When she was about to arrive at the location, she saw a police vehicle with red lights flashing following her, and she pulled over to the side of the road. The police informed her that she was driving ten kilometers per hour above the speed limit, so she received her first traffic ticket. She now believes that her feelings were conveying to her that this day was going to be a horrible day, but she could not put her finger on why until after she was cited.

I believe that to deepen our self-awareness, we need to revisit the major events that we have gone through in our lives. This may include buying a new home, the birth of a child, the death of a family member, the loss of a job, or the diagnosis of an illness.

I am convinced that if one looks at the time period prior to these significant life events, there were emotions and feelings that could be seen as a foretelling of what was to come. Being aware of these patterns will prepare us to be alert for and deal with similar situations in the future.

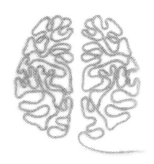

8

FEELINGS TELL WHEN ONE IS READY FOR A BREAK

My feelings in the warzone always told me when it was time for a break. Life in a warzone is always unpredictable, and everyday events dictate how people lead their lives. There can be no long-term planning since people live on a day-to-day basis. Life is characterized by constant stress.

There is always bad news: killings, ambushes, attacks, loss of property. The list is endless. Even taking a break does not mean much, because as soon as one comes back, the stress returns. It was also hard to take a break since I was alone most of the time and had no one to cover for me.

However, my body would always let me know when I was ready for one. For example, when I could not sleep anymore, when I heard very loud sounds and could not control my reactions, or if receiving bad news caused the left side of my body to ache constantly. Whenever I began to frequently experience these symptoms, I concluded that my body had had enough for a while, and it was time to take a break.

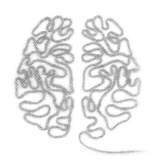

FEELINGS REVEAL HOSTILITY IN THE AIR

On one occasion, I talked to a Kenyan-born American to learn how his feelings have guided him. He recalled how during his first few months in America, he was a single man looking for a place to live. He found an apartment he could afford, but he did not really know the area. Whenever he dealt with fellow residents, he felt something was not right in their interactions, until he realized he was in an isolated and hostile neighborhood. I believe many of us have had a similar feeling when we have gone into a different city, an unfamiliar restaurant, or possibly walked in on a meeting where we did not know anyone and could feel the environment was hostile and we were unwelcome.

I will share with you one of my experiences when I came face-to-face with open hostility in a warzone. This happened in April 2003, when I went to Gulu on parish business. When I needed to return to Pajule, the only way home was to hitch a ride on a van that was going to be used to make contact with the LRA in the jungles of Koyo Lalogi.

I had no wish to meet the rebels. The plan was that the representatives of the Acoli Religious Leaders' Peace Initiative would take me to my parish and drop me off, and then the team would proceed to their rendezvous. However, they got nervous upon reaching the Pajule area and begged me to accompany them since I was the only religious leader among them. The delegation was made up of a traditional chief, an elder, and the driver of the vehicle. On their insistence, I accepted, even if I was not comfortable with my decision because travel plans in a warzone are strictly a personal affair—not driven by the company one is in or the sudden needs of the moment but by the directive of one's private and personal feelings.

When we reached the rebel base, the commanders looked surprised to see me, since they had previously been told how many people to expect. While they welcomed us and were courteous, I could feel their discomfort with my presence.

One of the commanders kept looking intently into my eyes to see my reactions. I remained calm and composed. It finally took the intervention of the local chief, who was part of the delegation, to reassure them that I was the priest in the Pajule parish and someone trustworthy. Eventually, they became comfortable with my presence.

The ability we had to feel the environment at the rebel base made us keep our meeting short and kept us continually mindful of what to say and how to say it. We did not attempt to make small talk with the rebels, unless they initiated it. We let the rebels take the lead in our discussions with them. We also avoided looking at our watches, so as not to signal to them that we were impatient or nervous and wanted to leave, yet we all wished for our time with them to end as soon as possible. The ones in charge of their communications were constantly in touch with other groups, asking about ground movements. We realized that while the commanders projected calm around us, those guarding them did not. Our feeling of safety in the company of the rebels was like an illusion. We dared not trust their behavior and feared that they could use any excuse to become violent and choose to detain us.

We were also afraid of an attack by government soldiers because we were now in the rebel company. Above all, our worst fear was that we had become hostages and prisoners, even if we were not in shackles.

Before we departed, I prayed with them and was careful to use words that could not be interpreted as making a judgment on their lifestyle. We left safely because our feelings had communicated to us about the situation we walked into.

I knew my decision to change my travel plans endangered my life because I was putting aside the directive of personal feelings, which was the reliable tool for good decision-making and safety for most of us who lived in a warzone. Fortunately, accompanying the delegation as a spiritual leader among them did not result in any harm to me.

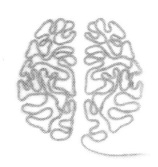

10

FEELINGS PROVIDE CLARITY WHEN FACED WITH TOUGH CHOICES

All human beings are faced with making difficult decisions. They review their first option and look at the pros and cons and then move on to the next one and the next and continue doing the same. After contemplating every possible choice, they may feel helpless. I faced several such situations while working in a warzone, but I was able to count on my feelings most of the time.

As a priest serving the Pajule area, I needed to travel to outlying stations, but my safety was always my immediate concern. No travel plans were ever final, and before setting out, I would ask myself if I should do it and then listen carefully to my feelings. If I felt at peace, I would start out, and if not, I would cancel my trip.

One morning, a man arrived at the parish early in the morning. He belonged to one of our chapels called Alim on the Lira road and informed me that their catechist was dying and that he wished to be anointed before he passed on.

I felt I could not turn down this request. The man had demonstrated real faith. He had taken a big risk to travel to the parish over the insecure roads. But if I were to go, there was no guarantee I would safely reach the place. To reinforce my courage, I went to the church. After I prayed, I still had no insight about how to proceed. It seemed that the best I could do was put everything in God's hands.

Since I leaned heavily toward going to Alim, I informed the parish staff that I intended to do so, even if there was a big risk I might not return. I then prayed together with the staff for my safety. After the prayer, one of the staff members asked me, "How do you feel inside yourself?" I told them that I felt at peace. This gave everyone confidence that I would be safe. The trip enabled someone to die in peace with God, so my decision to go to Alim was the right choice.

What one can learn from this is that when we do not have sufficient information about a difficult matter and need to rely on our feelings to make a decision, we need to develop a personal process to deal with the situation. The first step could be to review the choices and ensure we have considered every possible alternative. After that, we may need to consult our inner resources, which may be spiritual or religious. If a person identifies themselves as spiritual, perform a spiritual practice. If one is religious, pray to a higher power for help and guidance. After going through the first two steps, the final phase would be to consult one's feelings. If one feels inner peace with what one intends to do, it may be an indication that one can proceed, and if not, one may need to cancel or postpone what one has in mind.

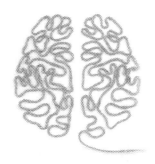 

THE POWER OF FEELINGS TO SHOW CARE FOR OTHERS

It is not always what is said that matters. Many times, people who are sick wish that their caregivers would show they understand and relate to their pain as they tend to their needs. I once talked with a person I will call John who told me about a visit to see a friend who was bedridden with cancer. John said he was glad to be there for him, but the hardest thing was that he did not know what to say when they were together. In fact, John did not have to say more than he needed. Just by being there, he showed that he understood the extreme emotional distress his friend was experiencing.

For example, one night, a patient was delivered to the hospital where I was stationed as a student chaplain, and after five minutes in the intensive care unit, the patient passed on. This family was known to the medical unit as one that reacted badly to difficulty, so a team of doctors and specialists was assembled to inform them of the loss of their loved one.

When they spoke to the family, the situation got out of hand. Some of the family members started to run around, while others banged the walls or began crying loudly. But what was most striking to me was the conduct of the medical team. In this chaotic situation, their focus was on explaining to the family both the medical procedures they had employed and the ones they would have wished to do. Yet it was clear to everyone else that no one was listening because the family members were in a state of shock from the sudden and unexpected death.

What the family needed was time and space to

mourn their loss. The best the medical team could do for this family was to feel their pain. This would not have required them to do or say anything. Many times, silence and presence are the only things families expect in such situations. By talking less and spending time with them, they can show the family that they understand their feelings of pain and can relate to them not only on a professional level but also on a human level.

On another occasion at the same hospital, I met a couple in the neonatal intensive care unit whose daughter was very sick. There was silence and so much sadness in the room. There was every evidence that their baby would not make it.

I felt sad for the baby, the couple, and the staff in the unit. But at the same time, I determined that the best way to show my concern and solidarity was to say very little. I greeted the couple, sat down, kept quiet, and joined them in observing their silence and sharing in their pain. After ten minutes, I said goodbye to them and left. There was no need for me to talk more than necessary, because I could not fix the situation or change it. The best I could do for the family was to let them know I was there for them and that I felt their pain.

Sometimes, this is a mistake people run into when faced with the illness of a friend, an acquaintance, or a family member. They talk too much, when only a moment of quiet and their presence is enough to convey that they care. To show that you feel someone's pain, you do not have to do something or say anything.

Three months later, this couple donated a set of chairs with the engraving "executive chairs" to the hospital in appreciation of the care their child had received. They insisted to the administration that I, the resident chaplain at the time, should be present to bless the chairs as they handed them over to the hospital.

When I again met the parents, I barely recognized them, but they remembered me very well. They told me that among the many visitors they had when their daughter was very sick, my visit and spending some quiet time with them was one of the most meaningful.

As I look back, I feel this visit was special for them because the couple felt through my silence that I shared in their pain and empathized with them. I believe that I was able to connect with them at a profound level that spoken words could not have achieved.

Regarding my own profession of hospital chaplaincy, the success of a chaplain depends on their ability to understand a patient through their own feelings. A chaplain may walk into a room, but the patient may not want to see him for many reasons. It could be that the patient is in pain, upset, tired, or not interested. Wishing to be polite, the patient may not be straightforward. Skillful chaplains are able to trust their gut feelings to discern what is going on in the patient's mind and decide whether or not to proceed with the visit.

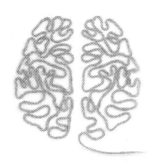

MY FEELINGS COMMUNICATE WHEN IT IS TIME TO MOVE ON

A hospital chief executive officer I will call Esther told me about how her feelings have guided and influenced her professional life. Esther told me that in order to become a chief executive officer in health care, she had held many different leadership roles. In each of them, she always listened to her inner feelings about when it was time to move from one position to the next.

My own experiences resonated with hers. When it has come time to make a career change or leave a position, I have always relied on my feelings. They have guided me in selecting places of employment, and when I settle in a workplace, I have no immediate desire to leave. Later, even if I have outgrown my position in an organization, the comfort and the relationships I have with other staff make me hesitant to explore opportunities elsewhere. I begin to look outside my organization only when my feelings begin to speak to me.

It often begins with a sudden feeling like an inner voice telling me that my time in a place is coming to an end. I also find myself getting more and more emotionally disconnected from the place. The activities I have been active in and passionate about become less fulfilling. Often, when I am confronted with the thought of moving on, I ignore it, but this thought will come back again and again and will not stop. Then, when I am with my colleagues for departmental events, I feel sad because I know that I will soon be leaving.

And when I walk in the hallways, I can also feel that my time is up. It is this constant reminder that my time in the place is coming to an end that forces me to start an active search for opportunities elsewhere. Eventually, I find a new home and move on.

There are many things that make people feel appreciated and happy to work for an organization. Here are some of them: good pay, a supportive management, good leadership, being part of a great team, and feeling that a person contributes to something greater than oneself— the common good. These are important for stability and satisfaction in a workplace, but they are not the only ones.

A person's feelings are also an important factor. A person's heart should be in the job, the work should give them a sense of personal accomplishment, and a person should feel personally liked and respected by their coworkers and superiors. If that is how a person feels, there is a higher likelihood that they will hold on to the job for a longer time.

In conclusion, an employee who intends to work for a substantial period of time for an employer must develop and maintain an emotional connection with their fellow employees and the leaders of the organization.

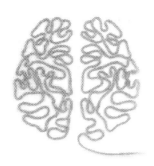

13

DOGS ALSO TRUST THEIR FEELINGS

When speaking of our four-legged friends one day, a salesperson I will call Gerald told me about his neighbor I will call Virginia, a lady in her late sixties who lived by herself with two dogs.

On one occasion, her son who lived in a nearby town visited her. Virginia told him that she was going to travel to a nearby shopping area. Unfortunately, she was involved in a head-on collision with another car, and this left her at a hospital in a state of shock and unable to contact her son until around eight o'clock that night.

Virginia informed him of her location, and the son wondered if the accident had occurred around four o'clock that afternoon. Virginia confirmed that it was indeed at four o'clock. The son remembered that at that very hour, the dogs began behaving strangely. They became restless and started barking furiously. They tore at the carpet on the floor and hit their heads against the wall. The son felt as if the dogs were attempting to give him a message, but he could not make sense of it. They did alert him to be aware that something was not right.

When I worked in the Pajule parish, I had a dog named Simba. He was very attentive to what was happening in the area. Since Simba was a security dog, he did not stay in the house. He had a place within the compound, and at night, he patrolled the grounds. If gunshots or loud blasts disturbed the night, Simba would sense the danger and run to check on me. If he did not hear me turning in my bed, a sign that I was still asleep, he would stand on his hind legs and bang the window sharply until I woke up. If he heard me turn in my bed, it was an indication to him that I was awake, and he would go and hide.

My maternal grandfather had a dog named Poppy. Poppy was a security dog and a hunting dog. He guarded my grandfather's home, as it had no wall fence. The village of Agoro in Northern Uganda had many wild animals roaming the area at night, and some of them were very good to eat. If Poppy heard the sound of an edible wild animal, he would seek it out, attack, and kill it. Then he would drag it home. Some of them were too big and heavy for Poppy to manage, so he would leave the catch in the bush and return home to get help. To pass his message, Poppy would sit in front of whoever was available and ceaselessly look directly into the face of that person while wagging his tail and making noise.

Then he would get up and walk out of the compound several times. Whenever people saw Poppy behave this way, it was a signal to them that he had slain something and it needed to be retrieved. They would promptly follow Poppy to the spot where the animal lay and bring his treasure and the next meal home.

I believe that cats, dogs, and pets in general have the capacity to connect with the feelings of human beings and communicate with them due to the close links they develop with people. I also think that people who have pets need to pay close attention to their behaviors in different circumstances because they are not always random actions. Sometimes, they are the very means with which they communicate important messages to human beings.

CONCLUSION

I conclude this book by calling for the integration of feelings and the intellect in our thought processes to avoid extremes. When most people make decisions, they lean more toward the intellect as a result of upbringing, social pressure, and the focus of the education they go through. There are also those who make decisions that lean more on their feelings. There is a problem with both these extremes.

I urge you to get in touch with your feelings. Good decision-making requires the integration of feelings and the intellect, because each of them contributes to the quality of a decision. You may be the product of an education that taught you to approach everything intellectually and to consider any expression of your feelings a sign of weakness and a lack of self-control.

As a result of the prejudices you might have developed regarding your feelings, you may have never gotten the chance to fully appreciate them. You may also work in a profession that is considered technical and encourages a general attitude that feelings do not count—such as accounting, engineering, and medicine. Just imagine how many years people spend in school, studying to develop their intellect, yet there is very little or no training to enhance human awareness of the range of their personal feelings.

To get in touch with one's feelings, one could even begin by asking oneself questions such as, "Why have I woken up feeling tired this morning?" The next step would be to ask, "When do I wake up tired?" It could be that I have a staff meeting every Friday afternoon, and this meeting is often contentious and emotionally draining. I believe this is the beginning of a person's self-awareness and gradual development of the ability to understand the range of one's feelings.

This is the manner in which an expert functions. An expert is a person who has a reservoir of knowledge and experience in a particular field that they can always turn to in order to be able to make the necessary associations and interpretations. People who have mastered their feelings can examine their life experiences and learn to make associations, differentiate patterns, and interpret situations to get meaning out of them.

The knowledge of the patterns of one's feelings is acquired through introspection—examining one's own mental and emotional processes. When I worked in a warzone, there were occasions that required me to travel, but I had no information at all about the safety of the road, so I had to examine and rely on my feelings. If they told me it was okay to travel, I did, and if not, I cancelled the journey.

All in all, I did not go into any detail about the intellect. First, the development of the intellect depends on and is supported by external means, such as our education in school, supplementary group learning, and regular reading. Second, it was not the focus of this book. But when it comes to being in touch with our feelings, it is a personal and an internal process. It is about being attentive to what is going on inside ourselves and learning the patterns, making associations, and drawing meanings from those experiences.

APPENDIX

Feelings and the Trump Phenomenon

I did not originally intend to include a part about President Donald Trump in this book, but as I paid closer attention to his statements and his conduct and behavior, I realized that in his everyday life, he follows many of the practices I advocate in this book. He is aware of his feelings, and he listens to them. He interprets them, and they guide his actions. Above all, he understands the patterns of his feelings and how they influence his decisions. However, while he has a strong mastery of his feelings, he is at the extreme end because he relies on them more heavily than his intellect.

Therefore, I wrote this section hoping to contribute

to the understanding of the thought process of the man Trump. While most people are guided by their intellect in their decision-making process, Donald Trump is primarily guided by his gut feelings. Understanding him is a great challenge for those who want to look at Trump through the lens of established practices, traditions, customs, and how previous presidents have behaved and conducted themselves while in and out of office.

When Donald Trump was a presidential candidate, and now as president of the United States, one of the main criticisms he has faced is that his decisions are rooted in his instincts and are not factually grounded.

Since my book is about a person's need to trust their feelings, I decided to look at President Trump's decision-making process. Indeed, my conclusion is that Donald Trump does rely more heavily on his feelings than his intellect, yet he is the president of a country that traditionally places the most value on using one's brain than following one's instincts.

I believe that this has led to some of the misunderstandings that President Trump has had with the media, since many of his decisions and choices do not seem to meet traditional guidelines and criteria.

When a US president speaks about a decision that has been made, the news media expects to get a detailed explanation of the process involved and the supporting facts. But for President Trump, it is his feelings that take priority. Some of the more concrete examples of his prevailing reliance on his gut feelings in his decision-making are the following:

President Trump's initial summit with the supreme leader of the Democratic People's Republic of Korea, Kim Jong Un—that he personally announced to the world in May 2018—was held the following month in Singapore, without any extensive prior preparation. In past American practice, presidents had only scheduled meetings with foreign heads of states after the ground work had been laid.

Another example is the seeming self-confidence of Mr. Trump that his face-to-face meetings with foreign leaders like Kim Jong Un of North Korea, Vladimir Putin of Russia, and Xi Jinping of China, who have a history of undermining US interests globally, would result in a change in their courses of action—that he would be the first US president to succeed where all others have failed.

The statements President Trump made weeks before his summit with the North Korean leader Kim Jong Un in June 2018 were very revealing of his approach to decision-making. When the press wished to know what he was doing to prepare himself for the meeting, his response was no surprise. He stated that making a deal with Mr. Kim was a question of attitude—his feelings toward something. From his answer, he indicated that he felt he did not to need to extensively plan or study the issues, because it was all about disposition.

At a later encounter with reporters, he said that if his feelings communicated to him that Kim Jong Un was not serious about the negotiations, he would walk out of the meeting. This statement confirms that Mr. Trump, in his decision-making process, is guided by his feelings and instincts rather than any serious considerations.

Another stark manifestation of President Trump's reliance on his gut instincts was seen at a news conference in Quebec, Canada. As he was leaving the G7 summit to travel to Singapore for his meeting with the North Korean leader Kim Jong Un, a reporter asked him how long it would take to figure out if Mr. Kim was committed to denuclearization. The answer the president gave clearly showed how important his gut feelings and instincts are to his decision-making process.

He said that he would figure out precisely what

President Kim Jong Un was seeking to get from the meeting within the first few minutes because of his own "feel and touch" at the moment—his way of analyzing the situation. He went on to say that people get to know if they like someone within the first five seconds of their first meeting, and he would know very quickly if something productive was going to come from his meeting with Kim Jong Un.

President Trump is unconventional because he leans more toward his feelings than his intellect in his decision-making process, and because of this, he has the freedom to do and say things that people holding or running for public office normally would not. I refer to his comments during the presidential campaign of 2016 that the late Senator John McCain was not a war hero because he was captured during the Vietnam War and that he preferred war heroes who had not been captured.

In the US, people or families that have sacrificed for

their country are considered to be sacrosanct, and this was clearly a derogatory statement. For most people, such utterances would have ended their political career. But I believe President Trump could act as he did because he trusted in his inner feelings and instincts. He must have felt similar patterns within himself, like in the previous disputes that he won. Indeed, his unconventional behavior, as outrageous as it may be to some, did not block his victory in the presidential election of November 2016.

My initial view that Donald Trump relies more on his feelings than his intellect came from watching him on television and reading his postings on social media. But to obtain a more complete picture of the man, I decided to read his book, *The Art of the Deal*, which confirmed my conclusions. Donald Trump, as a businessman and now president of the United States, indeed relies more on his instincts in his decision-making than his intellect.

Here are some examples from his book that show his

dominant reliance on feelings and instincts rather than his intellect. He has brought some of these tendencies to the presidency of the United States of America.

As he describes his daily work routine, President Trump says that he plays it very loose, does not carry a briefcase, and tries not to schedule too many meetings in one day. And he always leaves his door open. The reason is that he cannot be imaginative or inclined to take risks if he feels tied down by too much structure and prefers to come to work each day to see if any new opportunities arise or if anything critical needs his immediate attention. From a description of his normal workday, it should not be a surprise that establishing order and structure around him as president has been a great challenge for the staff in his White House.

In his book, Trump recommends that people should listen to their gut feelings no matter how good a business deal looks on paper. He recalls a time in his business career when a friend strongly urged him to invest in the oil industry, but as he considered the opportunity, he felt not inner peace but instead unease. The fact that he continued to have doubts about the opportunity made him decline. He went on to say that his uncertainties about the deal were soon confirmed, because within a few months, the well dried out, and all those who had invested lost their money.

In *The Art of the Deal*, Donald Trump also presents his philosophy for negotiations or dealmaking; he says that his style of dealmaking is very straightforward, for he will simply push and push until he gets what he is after. He believes that a person may be born with a genius for dealmaking, and while it requires some intelligence, what is needed most to succeed are instincts. He states that people who do not trust their instincts will never recognize their full potential because they do not have the courage to test them. And he reflects on the deals he has made in his business career: the ones that were a success, the ones that he lost, and the ones that he let pass. In all of them, he can see certain common elements or patterns—how he felt before a decision was made.

Further, he is convinced that he knows the market for his services and the tastes of his customer base. He says this makes it possible for him to provide them with exactly what they are looking to buy. Because of this, he does not hire "number crunchers" and does not trust "fancy" surveys. Rather, he does his own surveys in order to arrive at his own conclusions. As president, this tendency continues to manifest itself in his skepticism toward established institutions and professional bodies that people have esteemed for decades.

Donald Trump also provides another example for trusting his instincts from his own life experience. He states that when he started the Trump Towers building project on 725 Fifth Avenue, New York, the critics and reviewers did not support it because it stood for a lot of things that they were opposed to at the time. But when it was eventually completed, people liked it. And because of this, he will always trust his instincts.

Further, Mr. Trump reveals that his gut feelings are central to his inner decision-making process. He says that when he is thinking of buying a piece of property, he will ask people who live in and near the area what they think about the schools, the shops, and the crime rate. In another city, he may take cabs and talk to their drivers until he begins to get a gut feeling about whether to make a deal or not, and that is when he will make his decision.

While President Trump is deeply in touch with his gut feelings and is able to see common elements or patterns in the decisions that he has made, some of his personal actions and public policy show that he is weak in empathy. Trump failed to comfort Myeshia Johnson, the widow of La David T. Johnson, a soldier who was killed on a mission to Niger in Africa. It was reported that while the president was consoling the family, he told the widow that her husband knew what he had signed up for. He may not have intended to hurt the feelings of the grieving widow, but that was exactly what occurred.

Finally, his policy on hold regarding the separation of migrant children at the southern border from their parents when caught trying to illegally enter the country is another example of how little empathy he appears to have. While most people need to learn their feelings to understand them, I believe President Trump needs to learn to depend more on his intellect rather than his feelings, because it would provide order, structure, and predictability to his decision-making.

All in all, President Donald Trump still uses the same basic tools that worked for him in private life. As a businessman, he relied on gut feelings and instincts to make most decisions. During the years Trump will be president of the United States of America and occupy the White House, the intellect may occupy a back seat, but at least things will never be dull.

ABOUT THE AUTHOR

Dr. Robert Obol Nyeko was born in December 1971 in the Kitgum District of Northern Uganda. He is the firstborn of the nine children of Mary Tina Obol and Andrew P.K. Obol and is a Roman Catholic priest. Dr. Nyeko completed his training for the Catholic priesthood in his home country and was ordained a priest on August 18, 2001.

After his ordination to the priesthood, he was immediately assigned to serve as an associate pastor at Pajule parish, located in the archdiocese of Gulu. Of the three years he served in the parish before he came to the United States, only his first five months as a newly ordained priest proved to be peaceful. The rest were marked by war and violence when the Lord's Resistance Army (LRA) returned from their bases in South Sudan to Uganda to wage war and Pajule parish suddenly became the epicenter of the conflict.

This book on feelings has been motivated by his deep conviction that most people put little effort into mastering their own feelings, yet there is so much that they can communicate and reveal to us. When he worked in a warzone, most of the time there was not enough information available for him to think over things clearly, so he had to rely on how he felt about a specific situation and had to interpret what his feelings were telling him before he could make a decision.

Dr. Robert Obol Nyeko is a board-certified chaplain and a licensed nursing home administrator. Currently, he resides in Las Vegas, Nevada, and serves as a director of mission integration at a faith-based health system.

He holds a bachelor's degree in philosophy and sacred

theology from Urbaniana University in Rome, a master of arts in education from Walsh University in Canton, Ohio, and a master of arts in theology and a doctorate in ministry from Saint Mary Seminary and Graduate School of Theology in Wickliffe, Ohio. He has also completed a one-year residential training course as a hospital chaplain at the Cleveland Clinic in Ohio.

Dr. Nyeko has also taken courses offered in the master of business administration program at the University of Saint Mary, Leavenworth at the Overland Park Campus in Kansas. He has also been trained in administration and human resources at Johnson Community College at Overland Park in Kansas.

Printed in the United States
By Bookmasters